Encyclopaedia
Britannica
Educational
Corporation

Chicago/Toronto

Now You Know: How Animals Stay Alive

Library of Congress Catalog Number: 75-188518
International Standard Book Number: 0-87827-006-X

How Animals Stay Alive

Editorial Staff
Margeret Bjorck, Eth Clifford,
Barbara Donner, Anne Neigoff

Artist
James G. Teason

Consultants
G. Alan Solem, Curator of Invertebrates
Field Museum of Natural History
Chicago, Illinois

Deborah Partridge Wolfe, Professor of Education
Queens College, City University of New York
Flushing, New York

**Encyclopaedia
Britannica
Educational
Corporation**

Animals eat to stay alive.
Some animals eat plants.
Other animals eat the animals that eat plants.

Many animals eat other animals.
All day and night, wherever they live,
    animals are hunting for food.
While some animals hunt, other animals
    are hunting them.

How do animals stay alive?
How do they protect themselves from hunters?

Some animals run
        or jump
        or fly away
from the animals who hunt them for food.

Some animals try to run to a safe place
   when they are hunted for food.

The gopher runs into a burrow in the ground
   to get away from the coyote.
The coyote is too big to go into the hole.
In its burrow home the gopher is safe.

This mouse hunts for food in the fields.
While it is busy eating, an owl swoops low.
The owl is hunting for food, too.
The mouse runs as fast as it can.
It jumps into a hole in a log.
There it will be safe from the owl.

Colors help some animals to hide
from their hunters.

The colors of this young deer help it
to hide in the spring leaves.
When an enemy is near, the deer lies
still and quiet.
It does not move until the enemy
passes by.

This bird stays still on her nest
    when animals hunt her for food.
Is she easy to see in the leaves?

Shape and color help some animals to hide.

This grasshopper can be hard to see.
Sometimes it looks just like a green leaf.
Can you find it on the leafy twig?

The weed fish lives in the sea
where seaweed grows.
How does the way it looks help it to hide
from hunters?

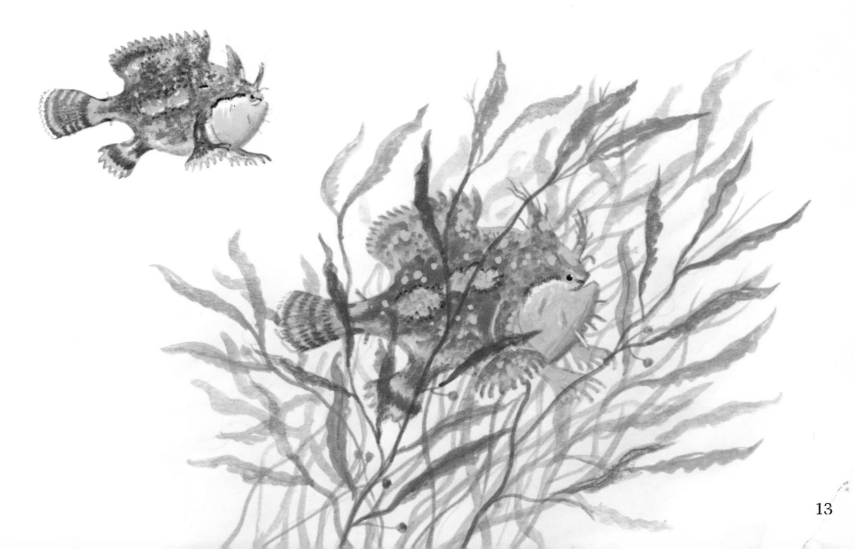

Some animals change color.
This is another way they hide from hunters.

What color is a chameleon?
When a chameleon is on a green leaf,
   it turns green.
When a chameleon is on a brown branch,
   it turns brown.
How does this help it to hide?

14

Some animals are one color in summer
and another color in winter.
The snowshoe hare has soft brown fur
in summer.
It turns white in winter, when the ground
is covered with snow.

15

Some animals fool the animals that hunt them
    for food.

When this moth is flying, you can see
    the colors on its wings.
How does the moth hide?
It folds its wings together and does not move
    as it rests on a tree trunk.
It looks like the bark of the tree.
Would you be fooled if you were hunting it?

Look at the bright colors of this jumping frog.
Plop! The frog lands on a leaf and is still.
The bright colors are hidden.
The frog is green with a few white specks.
The leaf is green, too.
Is the frog easy to see?

Other animals fool hunters in different ways.

The killdeer is hard to see as she sits
    on her nest.
But sometimes a hunter comes too near.
Then the killdeer flies away.
She flutters and cries as if she were hurt.
The hunter goes after her.
When the hunter is far away from the nest,
    the killdeer flies back to her babies.

18

The tail of this lizard helps it to get away
   from hungry animals.
When a hunter grabs the lizard's tail,
   the tail snaps off.
It wriggles and wriggles.
The lizard darts away and is safe.
Then the lizard grows a new tail.

Some animals have a bad taste or smell
that helps keep them safe from hunters.

The blue jay often eats butterflies,
but it will not eat this one.
The monarch butterfly tastes bad.
It can fly safely by when the blue jay
hunts for food.

A frightened skunk sprays its enemy.
The spray stings the eyes and smells bad.
Hunters soon learn to leave the skunk alone.

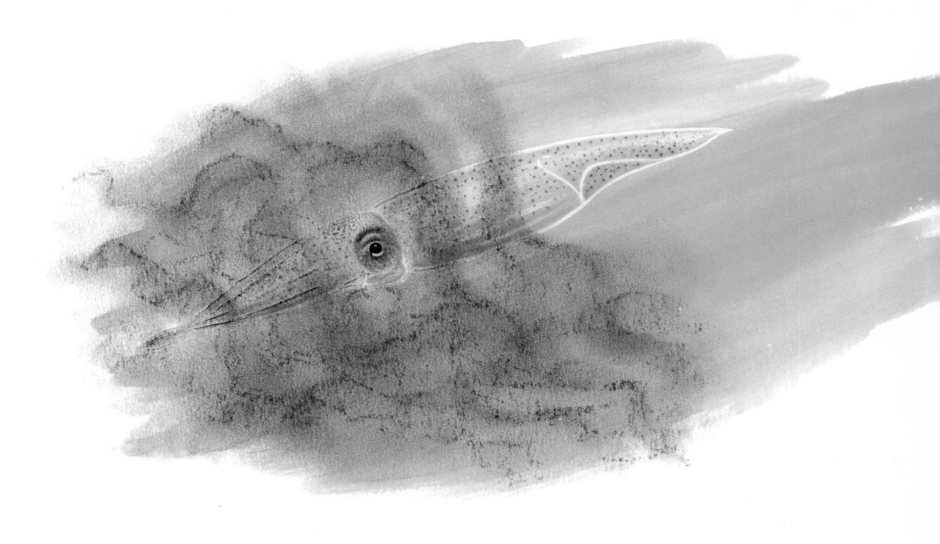

The squid keeps safe in a different way.
When it is in danger, it sprays a dark
   ink cloud around itself.
The hunter cannot find the squid.
The squid is safe.

Some animals have coverings that help
    keep them safe from hunters.

Sharp quills protect the porcupine.
When a hunter tries to bite a porcupine,
    the quills come off.
They stick in the hunter's mouth and paws.
This hunter will not try to bite
    a porcupine again!

22

The hedgehog has sharp spines on its body.
When danger is near, the hedgehog
    rolls into a ball.
The sharp spines stick out.
The hunter cannot bite it.

An armadillo is covered with hard plates like armor.
When it is frightened, it rolls into a ball.
The hard plates keep it safe.

This turtle has a thick shell.
When a hunter comes near, the turtle pulls
     its head, legs, and tail inside.

Many animals have colors and shapes
    that help them to hide.
Some animals hide from hunters.
Other animals hide as they hunt for food.

This fierce tiger hides in the tall grass.
It is hard to see when it is hunting.
Do you think the tiger often goes hungry?

This alligator looks like a log in the river
     as it waits for a bird to come near.
Then its sharp teeth snap!
The alligator has food to eat.

Some animals bite or sting the animals
    they hunt for food.
They bite or sting to protect themselves, too.

The bite of this snake has poison
    that can kill.
When an enemy comes near, the snake
    rattles a warning.
If the hunter does not stop, the rattlesnake
    will bite!
It will bite to kill animals for food, too.

A scorpion has poison in its sting.
It uses its sting to kill animals for food.
It stings its hunters, too.

Animals have many ways of trying to stay alive.
They hunt for food and are hunted by other animals.
People hunt animals, too.
If people kill too many animals,
    some kinds of animals may die out.
What can we do to help animals stay alive?

We protect some places so only animals
    can live and hunt there.
We have laws to keep people from hunting
    some kinds of animals.
Can you think of other ways we can help
    animals to stay alive?

31